HOW TO BUILD AN EDITORIAL BLOG

BUSINESS SKILLS FOR EDITORS: 2

Louise Harnby

CONTENTS

1. Introduction   1

   Overview   1

   Basic principles   1

   Why blogs work   3

   Avoiding blog death   3

   Value, stickiness and the power of emotion   4

   Business growth: Worth versus cost   4

   The slowish burn – beyond Google   5

2. Creating blog content   7

   Overview   7

   Content guidelines   7

   Focus on beginners   7

   Your audience's problems   8

   Don't puke over the reader   8

   The jigsaw puzzle   9

   Questions and polls   12

   Engage in forums and groups   12

   Repurpose and refresh   13

   Booklets   13

   Tip sheets and checklists   14

   Premium resources   14

   Rewrite old content   14

   Repurposing on other platforms   15

   Business repurposing   15

   Visual repurposing   16

   Analytics: refreshing or digging deeper   17

Send your content on holiday   17

Bring your guest content home   18

Invite guests   18

The Sales Lion framework   19

Create a series   20

'But someone else has already written this'   20

3. Branding your blog articles   22

Overview   22

A quick guide to building a compelling brand identity   22

Recognizability and trust   23

Images that inform   25

Headshot and/or logo   25

Colours   26

4. Your blog's home   28

Overview   28

Cost   28

Holism – trust and levelling up   28

Proximity – keeping the path unbroken   29

SEO benefits for your editorial business   29

Creating second homes – libraries and hubs   30

How content libraries aid navigation   30

5. Blog design and structure   33

Overview   33

Blog page – what to include   33

Individual posts – what to include   35

6. Blog promotion   42

Overview   42

Crafting promotion for social media   42

More promotion ideas 43

7. Keeping a content log 47
Overview 47
Why do we need a content log? 47

8. Scheduling your blog posts 51
Overview 51
How to approach the schedule 51
The scheduler 53

9. Subscription 55
Overview 55
MailChimp 55

10. Measuring success 57
Overview 57
Direct metrics 57
Indirect metrics 59

11. Does it work? 61

Tools and resources 62

1. Introduction

Overview

This guide is for those who want to hone their blogging skills and build a word-based content platform that compels clients to get in touch and drives visibility in the search engines.

Blogging is a powerful way to get noticed. We work with wordy people, and wordy people like wordy content.

I started blogging in 2011. I've made mistakes but I've got better at it and I'm still going. My blog is the single biggest driver of traffic to my website, not just for colleagues but for clients too. It's my hope that you'll be able to avoid the mistakes I made and make yourself visible more quickly by doing some of the things I wish I'd done earlier in my journey.

Basic principles

Underpin your blogging journey with the following in mind:

Create great stuff

Value trumps everything! If it's valuable, and solves problems, your blog content will survive all sorts of problems … from a few typos to changing algorithms and everything in between!

Post regularly and consistently

Your audience is more likely to tune in and engage with your blog content if you become known for solving their problems. Doing it consistently helps you to build trust and expectation such that people are more likely to subscribe and tune in. The more people who tune in, the more shares, likes, comments and links you'll receive. And that's great for your search-engine rankings and your referral rates from colleagues.

Google likes websites that are regularly updated. It shows that the business behind the website is active and providing a good user experience. And Google is democratic. It doesn't reward people based on whether their businesses are in the FTSE 500; it's more interested in rewarding interestingness. Blogging facilitates this. You're creating fresh stuff that people share, like and comment on, which gets you higher rankings. And that means that even the little guys like you and me get be findable for keywords if we make an effort. Working with Google is like making friends – if you're helpful and sociable, you get better results!

Move above the baseline

Most of us know a ton of editors and proofreaders who are highly trained and have a lot of experience. Training and experience are therefore baselines rather than standout qualities; you're just another editor among thousands online with a ton of skills and some pro qualifications.

If an author's looking for someone to help them with macro issues of story craft, who's going to wow them and inspire trust – the person who regularly helps them solve writing problems or the person whose website is all about the editor?

Colleagues are valuable too

Reputations aren't built overnight but if you consistently solve your colleagues' problems, over time people will remember you, and be grateful for the support you offer. They'll sign up to your blog or bookmark your site, and are more likely to comment when they're wowed by what you write.

That puts you top of mind for referrals and other opportunities such as speaking engagements (some of which might even been paying gigs). And if you create paid-for products such as books and courses, people are more likely to buy them because you've stablished trust. In short, we remember friends who help us out, not those who are always on the take.

Attend to quality control

We already know how difficult self-editing can be. That very fact keeps people like us in business. Still, the judgers are out there, so either pay one of your colleagues to check your work or buddy up with another blogger who posts a similar volume to you so you can carry out the quality control for each other.

Don't let the quest for perfection hold you back

Editors are more likely than most to worry about putting content out there that might not be perfect. Don't fret. Most people in our industry are incredibly kind and understand how much work goes into creating free, useful content. They'll tap you on the shoulder privately if they notice a typo!

If a bully does shame you in public for an error, please don't let it stop you. It's happened to me several times. Just fix the mistake and move on.

A few wee errors here and there in great content will be forgiven. Rude behaviour from a grunt won't be. You'll always be the winner, I promise.

Thinking about length

There's all sorts of research available about the ideal length of a blog post (and a video). Those stats are useful as guidance but quality will trump numbers every time. If someone has a problem and you can solve it in 250 words, great. If you need 2,000, that's fine too.

Why blogs work

We're editors and proofreaders. And given that we work with words, a written-content platform is the perfect way to demonstrate our wordy skills and knowledge to our colleagues and clients. Consider also the following:

- Blog posts are **scannable**. The busy reader can see at a glance the core themes that we're writing about.
- Unlike video, written information takes up **less bandwidth**, so if your reader's internet connection is slow, they'll still be able to access your content.
- Blog posts can be **captured, downloaded and printed**, enabling readers to access, annotate and store that content in ways that suit them rather than us.
- Blog posts can be **repurposed** in multiple wordy sways, which means we can satisfy a bigger audience without having to start from scratch.
- **Keywords** are discoverable in the search engines, which makes blog posts excellent for SEO.
- Blogs **build trust** because high-quality content that solves problems makes people feel grateful, that they're in safe hands, that they've learned something.

Avoiding blog death

Blog death usually happens for three reasons:

- The blogger runs out of ideas
- The quality of the content is not high enough to make it memorable

- The blogger struggles to make time for writing

If I've done my job properly, you will not run out of ideas for how to create compelling written and supporting audio-visual content. As long as you know who your audience is, what their problems are and how you can solve them, you'll be able to create blog content indefinitely.

As for finding the time, it's not just about looking at one issue, one time. Blog articles can be revisited, refreshed, repurposed and recycled, so you won't always be starting from scratch. The book also discusses scheduling and time-management techniques to keep you motivated and away from the rabbit hole.

Value, stickiness and the power of emotion

Blogging is a form of content marketing. The foundational principle is that of value – creating and delivering useful and usually free stuff.

When we help people by solving their problems, we make them feel something – grateful, thankful, relieved. In other words, we evoke emotion. Most people are more likely to remember how something or someone made them feel than specifically what was written or said. So when our content makes a colleague or client feel something, they're more likely to remember us long after they're done with that blog post or this video. Professional marketers call this memorability stickiness.

- If we stick in a potential client's head, we're more likely to be hired.
- If we stick in a colleague's head, we're more likely to be talked about, receive referrals, and have our content shared and linked to. Google uses that as an indicator of interestingness, which impacts positively on our rankings in the search engines.

Fabulous, valuable blog content that solves clients' and colleagues' problems makes our editorial businesses stickier and more discoverable.

Business growth: Worth versus cost

If we're stickier and more discoverable, we'll get more opportunities to quote for the kind of work we want to do at the price we want to do it.

Following is an email I received in early 2018. It's typical of the enquiries I receive.

Hi, Louise.

I'm writing to see if you might be interested in a job copyediting my novel.

I've been researching possible editors for a few weeks and have really enjoyed reading the wealth of material on your site. This is the start of my journey into the world of self-publishing and I was drawn to your experience in this area.

I'd love to get your thoughts on whether you think this would be a good fit for your editorial services.

If this sounds of interest, please let me know what you think and the best way to proceed.

It's absolutely not an indication that I'm better at my job than any other editor. Rather, it's an indication that my blog content makes me attractive to my core client group. Notice that the writer hasn't even mentioned money; he's already focusing on best fit ... which is exactly the mindset I want my potential clients to be in when they get in touch.

When we inspire trust and demonstrate expertise, we've already done a lot of the hard work. Our content makes good-fit clients concentrate on what we're worth rather than how much we cost.

And that means we don't have to worry one little bit about editors and agencies who are operating at the low-cost end of the market and competing on price.

It means we don't have to accept work from clients who are not ideal but who will do because that's preferable to an empty schedule.

The slowish burn – beyond Google

Blogging for business growth isn't a quick fix. We need to invest in the process so that we build a bank of findable, useful content over time. It can take two years or more to see significant results in the search engines. That being said, the burn might not be as slow as you think.

High-quality editorial directories act as shortcuts to being discoverable while you're building your search-engine rankings. Some national editorial societies work hard to make their member directories visible in the search engines. The Chartered Institute of Editing and Proofreading (CIEP) is a case in point.

If your professional association has a member directory but you're not in it, fix that as soon as you can; being findable in that is far easier than being findable in Google!

However, we still need to show potential clients why we're the best fit. An author browsing that directory and clicking through to member websites is still more likely to get in touch with you over 10 of your colleagues if you have amazing blog content that solves problems and evokes emotion.

If your national editorial society's member directory doesn't include links to member websites, begin lobbying them for a change immediately. And if your society isn't actively promoting itself and its directory online, ask them why not and when that's going to change!

2. Creating blog content

Overview

To keep our blogs vibrant so that they continue to drive traffic to our websites and generate business leads, we need to keep the content flowing.

Don't forget that we're trying to make people *feel* something, and solving problems is a sure-fire way to evoke emotion. That's what makes us memorable, and what keeps our blogs sticky. Plus, the search engines love regular content so it's good for your SEO.

Here are some ideas to help you create content and keep your blog blooming!

Content guidelines

Create great text. Cite any primary sources, of course; we, as editors, know better than anyone the problems of plagiarism and the etiquette of citation. Here's the guidance I use for creating content (based on the advice of pro white-paper writer Gordon Graham):

- Think like a lawyer
- Research like a think tank
- Cite like a scholar
- Write like a journalist
- Communicate like a person

Focus on beginners

There will always be more beginners than pros so don't shy away from creating blog content that appeals to those who are at the start of their journey. There's nothing wrong with assuming your readers know nothing. And if you omit the basics because you're concerned about boring an advanced reader, you'll lose the opportunity to solve problems for a chunk of potential clients.

Your audience's problems

Some of the blogs I wrote between 2011 and 2015 are a technical disgrace but they worked – and still work – because the content is helpful (based on solving problems) and shareable.

Why it needs to be about them

A blog that doesn't solve problems is a written exercise in self-indulgence and won't make us the go-to professionals for anything. At best, we'll be instantly forgettable; at worst, people will talk about us for all the wrong reasons.

A colleague recently told me about a piece of video content he'd watched: 'Talk about me-me-me. After 10 minutes I'd lost the will to live. After 20, I'd lost the will for the vlogger to live.' I trust my colleague, whereas I don't know or trust that vlogger. Consequently, I didn't watch the video.

Great problem-solving content is *evergreen* – meaning it stays relevant for eons. That means it's shareable for eons. All the effort you put in to creating a single blog post can be used again and again.

Don't puke over the reader

There are a ton of online examples of desperate business owners employing attention-seeking methods to get eyes on their content. It can work once, maybe twice. But if we rely on shock, surprise, upset or gaining sympathy, and don't provide a solution, our content marketing won't work.

We all have problems – that's doesn't mean we have to vomit over our audience with our content. Plus, shock and controversy have a short shelf-life. Today's audiences are easily desensitized and quickly bored, so high-quality problem-solving content will trump the shock factor every time.

Nothing should appear on our blogs that doesn't help the reader move forward in some way. And if we can't solve a problem, we should hold off, research and rewrite. Only once we have a solution should we publish.

When we do solve problems, we make ourselves valuable. People are more likely to talk about, share, like and comment on our blog content. And that has huge SEO benefits over time because the search engines love seeing evidence of a great user experience. Focus on solving the audience's problems from the get-go and we will be well on the way to building a platform that puts us top of mind and discoverable in the search engines.

The jigsaw puzzle

Your target audience and the relevant, sticky, valuable content that solves their problems are like two adjacent pieces of a jigsaw puzzle. Get the match right and there'll be no stopping you.

Audiences fall into two broad categories:

- Colleagues
- Potential clients

Colleagues

This audience comprises your fellow editors, proofreaders, indexers, copywriters and translators. They are your advocates. Even though this group won't necessarily buy from you (unless you're selling training or business guidance) they are still powerful, not least because the global editorial community is possibly the most generous group of people on the planet! Colleagues will read, comment on, share, link to, talk about and recommend your posts. And that's great for your SEO.

They'll also remember you. And that means when they're looking for someone who offers an editorial service that's outside their skill set, you're more likely to receive a referral.

All of us are more inclined to put work leads in front of people who help us, who solve our problems, who make our lives easier, and who demonstrate knowledge and skill. I don't touch scientific or legal editing with a barge pole and so when that work is offered to me, it's the colleagues who are top of mind that get the referrals.

I discovered a developmental editing colleague via her great blog content. And because she demonstrates her artistry clearly through her blog, I don't hesitate to refer writers who come calling with a request for story editing.

Plus, even if you're blogging for colleagues, you're creating regular fresh content with keywords that are likely to be used when clients are doing Google searches. For example, my colleague-focused posts on editing pornography and sourcing proofreading training have helped to make me visible in the search engines for keywords that my potential clients use to search for help with editing adult material.

Specialist knowledge

If you have a specialism, create content that demonstrates your skill to your colleagues. Examples might include the following:

- How do I become a medical editor?
- What are the best training courses for life-science editors?
- What's the difference between legal editing and legal proofreading?
- How do I get work with fiction publishers?
- 8 tips for proofreading academic theses and dissertations

Your skill might lie in other areas. I worked in a marketing capacity before I set up my editorial business and I turned that knowledge, and my passion for it, into a niche that I often blog about (and now create training courses about) because it's valuable to those who have different knowledge bases, experiences and passions.

Consider the following:

- If you're a former lawyer, you could dedicate a chunk of your blog content to terms and conditions, kill fees, editing contracts, liability, insurance, copyright, privacy, and intellectual property rights.
- If you're a former accountant, you could focus some of your content on taxation, business set-up, deductions and expenses, pension provision, health insurance, money-saving tips, record keeping, and accounting software.
- If you're a former therapist, you could focus on helping your colleagues have healthier freelance lives: taking breaks, relaxation techniques, stress relief, dealing with anxiety, depression and loneliness, conquering fear, managing difficult clients, and overcoming client rejection.

Potential clients

This audience is the most important. It's the people you want to sell to – those for whom you edit and proofread. I believe that editors and proofreaders have the best chance of standing out in the market when they specialize. A potential client is far more likely to choose someone who oozes experience and passion for a subject (or related group of subjects) than a generalist whose message is 'I can edit anything'.

So what's your specialism? And who is most likely to hire you based on that skill set? Examples might include:

- First-time self-publishing authors of fiction
- Small-business owners
- Non-native English-speaking academics submitting to scholarly English-language medical journals
- Law students, practising lawyers, and legal scholars
- Engineers and other technicians

The problems faced by the people in each of those examples will be very different and should be the focus of your blog content. That way, when they visit your site, you can show them that you're already under their skin.

Specialist knowledge

A blog full of musings on the difficulties of setting up a freelance business is not going to inspire nurses who need their dissertations proofreading, but articles that advise on structuring medical and healthcare writing, submitting to nursing journals, self-editing dissertations, balancing study and practice, and conventional grammar, spelling and punctuation will.

Here are two more ideas for regular blog content that would help specific audiences.

- **First-time self-publishing authors of fiction:** Dialogue tagging and punctuation; showing and telling; dangling modifiers; creating EPUB files; copyright and song lyrics; the different levels of editing; how to source professional editors; guidance on working with agents.
- **Small-business owners:** Distilling complex material into plain English; how to create effective lists; how to structure reports; grammar, spelling and punctuation conventions; gender-inclusive language; using style guides; writing for the web; basic SEO guidance; keyboard shortcuts.

Workaday cues – what you spot

When you're editing and proofreading, and you spot a client coming unstuck repeatedly, that's your cue to blog about the issue. After all, if they've struggled, it's likely that another writer has too. Examples you might have come across include:

- Problems with dialogue tagging
- Confusion over how to create in-text citations according to a given style manual's preferences
- Confusion over the different levels of editorial intervention

And pay attention to the questions clients ask you. In 2017, four authors asked me whether it was necessary to hire an editor if they planned to submit to an agent. I wrote a blog post about the issue and turned it into an ebooklet that sits in my website's self-publishing library. I know that content is on point because members of the target audience asked the question.

Questions and polls

Invite people to email you with questions – colleagues and clients. Though only one person has asked that question, there's a good chance that many others have wondered the same thing.

Place a button at the end of each blog post, or in the sidebar of your blog page, or content hub page to that it's clear that you welcome this level of interaction.

Inviting questions is a powerful way of creating personal engagement with your audience because you're offering direct contact and a form of free consultancy.

Ask your own questions and create polls on your social media channels (or email colleagues or clients), then curate the responses in a blog post. Acknowledge the contributors in the article and tag those people when you share the article via your social media channels. You're more likely to get shares and likes from the contributors, which is great for SEO and audience reach.

Engage in forums and groups

Forums aren't just great for networking; they're excellent blog content generators. Every question that a colleague asks in an online forum or group, or a local-networking meeting, is an opportunity for a blog post.

If you don't know the answer to the question, but you think the solution would fit well within your blog's focus, do the research and find an answer that you could turn into an article.

Some of my rates-focused articles came out of concerns aired in an online Facebook group and the Chartered Institute of Editing and Proofreading (CIEP) forum. And I have colleagues who've created blog content based on questions that were asked in the Alliance for Independent Authors forum.

Repurpose and refresh

Repurposing works both ways – you can create blog articles from existing content located elsewhere, and you can create different forms of content from your blog posts.

Think about your knowledge and skills, and what your audience will find useful. Is there information that would be usable in another form and that could be repurposed using existing content? Examples might include:

- Citation guidelines summary sheet
- A list of handy find/replace strings in a tip sheet
- A written tutorial that would work well as a screencast (or vice versa)
- A series of articles that could be pulled together in an ebook

'Bring Your Guest Content Home' looks at how you can repurpose guest blog articles; you can extend this to your conference presentations, magazine articles and training workshop slides too. If you own the copyright, the content is yours to repurpose on your blog in whichever form you choose.

Booklets

Booklets are effective because not everyone wants to access content in the same way. Blogs require the reader to bounce around the archives to find what they want.

Make things easier – grab related content (say from a series or using your content log) and put it all in one place. That way, your reader doesn't have to work so hard to get everything they need.

If you've created a booklet first, divide that up into separate blog posts. I did this with my *Guidelines for Authors* ebook. After publishing it, I lifted three sections and used them as individual blog posts:

- 'What's the difference between a rule and a preference?'
- 'What's a style sheet and how do I create one? Help for indie authors'
- 'Beginner fiction writers – 8 tips to stop you stumbling'

Tip sheets and checklists

You can create blog posts that are short on text but big on value. Create and include a free downloadable checklist or tip sheet. I did this with 'Proofreading checklist: How to check page proofs like a professional'. It's a popular post with a useful tool that's garnered over 5,500 page views and hundreds of downloads via my blog and the chatbot campaign I carried out on Facebook.

Premium resources

Turn your blog content into premium resources, free and paid.

If you want to encourage sign-up to your blog or mailing list, consider creating free lead magnets, rather than just giving it all away at the point of entry.

Sophie Playle uses this approach. Because readers are required to disclose a minimal amount of information (their email address) in return for the freebie, her subscription list is full of people who are serious about what she's offering. The numbers become important if you're using MailChimp and you want to remain in the free plan; you don't want people on your list who aren't reading your content.

Rich Adin has gone one step further. He's taken a large chunk of his free blog content and repurposed it as a book. Published in 2013, *The Business of Editing* is a 462-page tome collating over 80 articles on pricing, start-up guidance, software, and the levels of editing.

It's actually an enormous collection of blog articles but it makes people's lives easier because they can access the content in one place and he's structured it by theme. It's also available in paperback, which means it's structured accessibly and logically, whereas the blog is structured by date of article publication. For many, that's worth $25 because they can dip in at their leisure and don't need a device to access it. I took a similar approach with my book *Editing Fiction at Sentence Level*.

Rewrite old content

If you have older content that's gone out of date, feels a little stale, or you've had a rethink, rewrite from a new angle.

In 2013, I wrote an article called 'Editorial freelancing – putting your eggs in more than one basket.' I revisited that piece and decided that while I was satisfied with it in the main, the advice on how to solve the problem was a little thin.

I decided to write a new article that addressed the same issue but focused more on solutions. The result was 'When one client isn't enough – emergency marketing for editors and proofreaders'. To make it stand out from the original post, I included an ebooklet: the SOS Editorial Marketing Strategy'. My readers loved it – over 4,700 page views and hundreds of downloads. One reader even emailed me to say that the strategy in the booklet had enabled her to pay that month's mortgage.

Again, it's an example of using a blog to create something that helps solve a problem – and that's always going to be a winner. If you can rewrite old content and make it better, don't hesitate to do so.

Repurposing on other platforms

Stretch your blogging efforts by republishing posts on Facebook, Twitter and LinkedIn. This can be valuable because social media algorithms reward those who keep people on the platform's land. When you upload content direct to a platform (this is referred to as native uploading) you play to the algorithms' preferences and the platforms will push your content in front of more people's faces via their newsfeeds. And that means you can get eyes on your blogs posts from outside your existing network.

Here are a few things to bear in mind:

- You retain the copyright on any content you upload to social media.
- Leave at least a week before uploading so that Google has time to assign authority to the original post on your website.
- Create a different title so that the post is findable different ways in the search engines.

Business repurposing

Think about how you might repurpose your blog content for business use. My two favourite ways of using blog posts in my business is as follows:

- **Editorial reports:** Link to blog posts that deepen a client's understanding of the *why* of your edits, and demonstrate your editorial excellence.

- **Quotes:** Link to blog posts that demonstrate your knowledge in instil trust in a potential client. It'll make your quote stand out.

Visual repurposing

Pictures and video are two additional ways of repurposing your blog content so that it's accessible to people with different preferences. I recommend having text versions of the content, too, because some people still prefer to read instructions (and will even go so far as to print useful blog posts) and because the keywords will help to make you discoverable in the search engines.

Visual repurposing takes a lot more effort than the other methods outlined. But the impact makes you stand out because it's done infrequently in our market.

Here are some options to consider:

Slideshows

A good alternative for written content that's educational. Create your slideshow in PowerPoint, record the show (and your voice) using the onboard tools, and save it as an MP4. Run it recording through Handbrake to shrink the file size and upload to YouTube.

Screencasts

Great for demonstrations of how to use a tool (for example, using Word's styles palette or installing a macro).

Infographics

These allow readers to access a key message without having to read all of the blog-post text. Including them appeals to the reader who's short of time.

Video

Video shows the editor behind the text. Even a 1,500-word blog post can be condensed into a 10-minute video, or just listened to (like a podcast). That means it's accessible to readers on the go, those who want to be able to do other things while they're on your blog.

Analytics: refreshing or digging deeper

Once you've built up a bank of content, look at your analytics to find out what's performing well. Then dig deeper and create more of it ... perhaps refreshing outdated content, or digging a little deeper.

Case study: Proofreading stamps

Some years ago, I wrote a blog that included free downloadable files of PDF proofreading stamps. The post was popular – Google Analytics told me so. It also generated discussion and questions. So I dug deeper into onscreen proofreading, and over time created the following articles:

- 'Semi-automatic Stamps Upload in PDF-XChange Viewer'
- 'Onscreen proofreading – a freelance perspective (guest article for Out of House Publishing)'
- 'Six tips for drama-free onscreen proofreading'
- 'Onscreen proofreading tips: Reorganizing your stamps palette in PDF-Xchange'
- 'PDF proofreading – essential first-step checks': This was republished by BookMachine some months later and included in their annual publishing collaboration with Kingston University Press: *Snapshots: New Notes on the Publishing Industry*. It demonstrates how your editorial blogging might take you in directions you never envisaged.

Send your content on holiday

Guest blogging should not be underestimated. Think of it as sending your blog content on holiday!

Guesting gives you the opportunity to get your blog content in front of a new audience. If like me, you tend to guest for editors, there'll be a lot of audience overlap, but it's still a signal to your community that others value your writing.

Think not only about colleagues for whom you could write but bigger publications. If you're a legal, medical or technical editor, are there industry magazines or journals that you might submit to?

Given that lawyers, medics and engineers write for these publications, chances are they'll need a qualified editor to assist them. What better way to get on their radar by publishing an article that explains how to source, assess and brief one?

If you decide to hit a big publication, give your very best to the content:

- Check the tone of the articles so that you hit the right notes.
- Check the submission guidelines to ensure you meet the criteria and fulfil the brief.
- However much effort you normally put into a blog post, triple it.

Bring your guest content home

Someone asks you to write a blog post for them. You're happy to oblige – you respect them and their business, understand the SEO benefits provided by the links between your sites (via the bio that's included), and appreciate the expanded audience reach.

You're proud of that article ... so much so that a part of you wishes it was on your own site! It's time to bring it home. That way you can create new content for your own blog with little additional effort.

Don't just replicate that blog article on your website; tweak it with a new title, fresh images, and make sure it's up to date.

Creating a gift

If you're short of time, there's a simple solution: turn your guest post into a downloadable PDF booklet. You'll be offering something of value that your reader can take away – a gift.

I create my booklets in Google Slides. Then I download the content as a PDF and run it through TinyPNG to reduce the size. For the 3D-effect cover image I use Boxshot.

Invite guests

It's likely that you'll have some ideas for content that would solve your clients' problems but don't have the expertise to create the solutions. You could do the research and create the content yourself. However, that's time-consuming. Instead, collaborate and use the guest to water your blogging garden!

It's a great promotional opportunity for them, too, and if you can reciprocate, all the better. Plus, there's the potential for both of you to reach new audiences.

Case study 1: The publisher

Chris Hamilton-Emery is the co-founder of Salt Publishing and The Cover Factory. He wrote a guest article for me that guides self-publishers on creating a standout book cover.

Case study 2: The military editor

Steve Allen is a US book editor and former soldier. He has knowledge about firearms that I don't. After commenting on one of blog articles, I asked him if he'd be interested in guesting. He wrote a 6,000-word piece on firearms and fiction, which I turned into a blog series and a booklet.

Case study 3: The voice artist

Ray Greenley is a voice artist who helps self-publishers create audiobooks. I found Ray on Twitter and asked if he'd like to write a guest post for me. He obliged with over 5,000 words. I turned this into a 5-part blog-post series and a booklet.

Case study 4: The author

Jeff Carson is a full-time indie author of crime thrillers, and one of my clients. He agreed to write an article about his top tips for earning a living from being a self-published fiction author.

The Sales Lion framework

Marcus Sheridan, The Sales Lion, believes there are several broad topics that are core drivers of traffic and leads. Using this framework, you can create a lot of blog title ideas! I came up with enough ideas to fill a two-year weekly publishing schedule in under an hour, then whittled it down to those relevant only to my particular audience.

I'm confident you'll be able to do the same. Below are the categories, each with one example.

- **Who/which/where:** For example, who publishes social science books and do they work with freelance editors and proofreaders?
- **Problems:** For example, how do I use Track Changes?
- **Cost:** For example, how much does proofreading cost and why?
- **Reviews:** For example, a review of BELS membership
- **Comparisons and differences:** For example, self-publishing vs going through an agent. What's the difference?

- **Recommendations**: For example, what are best online proofreading and editing courses?

Create a series

Series are another good option because they allow us to create content in batches. Furthermore, because the blog posts are related, you're not starting from scratch each time; you're already in the right headspace so you'll likely be able to create the content faster.

Series enable you to dig deep but spread out your blog content over time.

'But someone else has already written this'

You're solving the problems of people who've bothered to visit *your* website, not someone else's. If a reader can't solve their problems with you, they'll go elsewhere. Your blog should demonstrate your willingness and ability to provide solutions, so if you need a piece of content on your site, *you* should create it. It will be original in that it will be imbued with your brand identity, your angle, your voice.

Put an American, a Brit, an Aussie and a Canadian in the same room and ask them to speak English. They'll understand each other well enough even though their accents differ. Well, we bring our own accents to our blogs too. Remember the Content Guidelines at the start of this chapter and you won't go wrong.

For you to do ...

First, make a note of what you already know. This will save you time when creating some of your content. Think about:

- The work you've already done.
- What the clients' problems were.
- Your previous work experience.
- Your educational background.
- The demands in your life and how you solve those problems.
- What you've learned so far from conferences, career experience, and life experience. Can you tweak that knowledge in a way that solves your clients' problems?

Record your ideas about how you're going to create regular content for years to come:

- Who is your audience?
- What are their problems and how can you solve them?
- If you don't know what their problems are, how will you find out? Think about forums, groups, social media and the problems you see in your work.
- How can you increase your productivity by repurposing content?
- Make a note of content that you could divide into several related posts in the form of a series.
- If you're already creating content, look at your analytics and make a note of what's working well and what you might therefore do more of.

3. Branding your blog articles

Overview

Your blog is a business tool and should therefore look like it's part of your stable. The overarching message is that you're an editor with a ton of expertise who's willing and generous enough to solve problems for free. That leads to trust.

With recognizable branding, you can build additional trust by reinforcing the connection between your business and your free content. It makes the jump from your other website pages to your blog, and back again, feel seamless.

A quick guide to building a compelling brand identity

A strong brand needs to incorporate our core brand values so that our clients know what they're doing on our website and why they should bother staying there. Brand values are what we use to mould people's perceptions of us.

We want clients to visit our websites and glimpse certain compelling attributes. Not boring stuff like how we meet deadlines and are professional and trained. Those things are important ⌐⌐ of course they are – but they're not unique. None of us should be operating unless we're professional, trained and can meet our deadlines. Instead, we want them thinking about the next level.

My brand values are:

- professional Labrador
- elegant editor
- self-publishing advocate

I try to convey those things with everything I offer on my website … from the resources I create on my blog and funnel through to my content hub, to the style of my headshot. The stuff about me and my history is right at the bottom of my home page.

To develop your own set of core brand values, think deeply about:

- The things you value, the kind of person you are, and what you want people to say about you when you're not in the room.

- Who your perfect client is and what they're worried about.
- How the person you would never want to be (anti-you) thinks and presents themselves online.

When you're thinking about the kind of person you are, don't be afraid to include things that you might perceive as negative or embarrassing; you can turn these into positives when you're developing your brand identity.

For example, I'm rather oversensitive and moved easily to tears even by advertisements. This can be handy for an empathetic fiction editor! By developing a brand identity, we're able to focus more keenly on how best to represent business and our content so that's they're unique, authentic and recognizable to the clients and customers we most want to attract.

Recognizability and trust

Recognizability is a fast-track to engagement. This shouldn't come as a surprise. Who are you more likely to open your front door to? The person you recognize or the stranger? When your colleagues and clients see links to your blog content on third-party platforms they respond in the same way. If they don't recognize the content they'll think twice before sharing.

That issue of recognizability becomes more important when we consider promotion. You will be promoting your blog content otherwise it will be invisible, and therefore of no economic value to you. To make your blog visible in the search engines and memorable in your colleagues' minds, it needs to have eyes on it in the first place – and those eyes will lead to likes, shares and retweets, as well as links to and discussions about your content.

That means you'll be linking to your content elsewhere, not least on social media. And given that social media and the search engines will pull partial text and images from your posts, it's essential that it's identifiable as yours if you want it to work hard for you.

Plus, once you're trusted, people will share and re-share your blog content even without reading it first. Now, I know this doesn't sound like good practice, but it happens and there's no point in burying our heads in the sand over the issue. The reason it happens is because they're massively busy and it's a way for them to demonstrate to their own audience that they're engaged reciprocators without having to spend valuable time reading every single thing that comes in front of their noses.

The more recognizable your blog content is the greater the engagement and the harder it will work for you in terms of making your business visible.

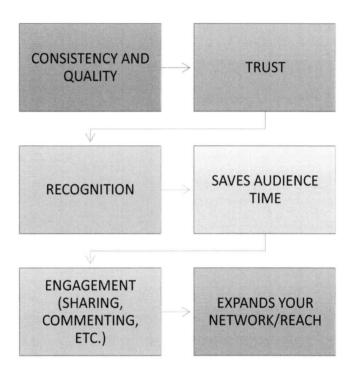

Recognizability via voice

All editors have to pay attention to voice, whether we work with fiction, academic texts or business content. Your own business has a voice too, one that reflects your personality and your business values. Voice is part of brand identity and we need to pay attention to it in our blog posts.

Aim for **consistency** in the main. If your voice tends towards warmth and hand-holding and you introduce a sweary rant into your blog bank, readers will wonder what's going on! It's not that the topic you're writing about isn't deserving of a sweary, ranty tone, but that it might make you sound like someone else – and that person is different from the one who's trusted by your existing readership. In other words, it's off-brand.

Have a think about your blog tone. What elements of your business's brand identity do you want it to convey? Examples might include the following:

- Introspection
- Cheekiness
- Scholarliness
- Brevity and clarity
- Dreamy and emotionally responsive
- Controversy

It's not about right or wrong but about how you want to make people feel when you blog and how you'd like to be perceived by those you want to compel.

Images that inform

Think about how you might brand the images in your blog posts so that they become recognizable to your audience. If you're consistent, people will know that those blog posts are yours before they've even seen your name. If you're trusted, people will be more likely to share the content quickly, perhaps without even reading it. These kinds of images work brilliantly not only for readers already on your blog but also those deciding whether to click through from social media.

Here are two examples of consistent, recognizable branding from the editorial and writing blogging community:

Sophie Playle, editor

Joanna Penn, writer

Headshot and/or logo

Might you incorporate your official headshot and logo into your posts' header images so that people can see immediately that it's your content?

Here's are some examples of informational click bait and headshots combined. In one example, the blogger has created an avatar using Bitmoji, rather than a headshot, to brand his blog posts consistently.

Louise Harnby, editor

Amanda Webb, small-business blogger

John Espirian, technical writer

Colours

If you don't know your brand colours, identify them. If you don't have any, decide on some! That way you can bring consistency and recognizability to your blog-post images.

- A quick tip – if you want lighter hues, change the opacity not the colours themselves.
- Use a hex–RGB converter to keep your brand colours standard across different platforms (e.g. Twitter and my Weebly-hosted blog use hex. Microsoft Office uses RGB). I recommend Yellowpipe because it converts both ways – from hex to RGB, and RGB to hex.
- Think about the emotions that colours might evoke: more muted hues could be soothing, primary colours could be energising, and dark colours could add an air of mystery!

- Create a bio page on your website. You can use it to store your official suite of headshots, a logo, a short description, your brand colours, and your social media profiles. This provides a one-stop shop that you can refer others to when they want to link to you on their own blog (or other content channel).

For you to do ...

To recap, when branding your blog, consider the following:

- Your brand identity – what are you all about and with whom are you trying to build trust?

How will you reflect this? Consider:

- The colours for banners, images, headers, buttons and links.
- Your voice and the way you want people to perceive you and the emotions you'd like to arouse.
- The design of the images that help the reader understand what's on offer and why they should bother.
- Your headshot or avatar.

4. Your blog's home

Overview

Every blog needs a good home! You have a choice about where to host it – it can be a separate entity or it can sit on your business website. My recommendation is that when you're blogging for business growth, you place it on your editorial business website. There are four reasons behind my thinking:

- Cost
- Holism – trust and levelling up
- Proximity – keeping the chain unbroken
- SEO benefits for your editorial business

Cost

If you host your blog separately, you'll need to build in extra budget to maintain it – stuff like a custom domain name, the price of hosting, and any plugins you buy. Then there's the cost on your time – not only will you have to devote time to making your business website visible, but your blog too. Actually, though, this is the least important reason for hosting the two together ...

Holism – trust and levelling up

By hosting your blog on the same platform as your editing services, you're reinforcing a core message: that you're a trustworthy editor who also solves problems for free. That's a far more powerful proposition than being a blogger who happens to have an editing arm.

Let's go back to first principles for a moment.

Your blog is not a standalone entity. It's a marketing tool that demonstrates your expertise, your willingness to engage and your ability to solve problems. Remember, when we solve problems we make people feel something. Whether that's grateful, relieved, happy, empowered, confident, able to move forward, or something else, those emotions are powerful. They make you and your blog memorable, something worth talking about, linking to, sharing, revisiting and bookmarking.

If you do it regularly, such that you become someone who won't let them down, you're on your way to instilling trust.

Then, when a client is ready to level up by commissioning work that they feel is outside their own skill set, they'll be more inclined to go to someone trustworthy, someone who helped them but asked for nothing in return ... someone whom they regard as first and foremost an editor because all that trustworthy, sticky stuff is right there on your business website.

Proximity – keeping the path unbroken

Once you've built trust, you need to make it as easy as possible for the client to move from your free blog content to your paid-for service content. If your blog is on another site, you force the client away from the goodies and onto a new platform. That breaks the path between your service content and your valuable freebies. You introduce distraction.

Keeping things in one place puts your editorial services, your contact page and your blog content front and centre, and allows the client to move from one to another with minimum effort.

SEO benefits for your editorial business

Blog posts are full of rich keyword juice that make you visible in the search engines. For example, if you regularly include keywords such as proofreader, editor, editing, and academic proofreading in your blog articles, your website will develop keyword authority for those terms. On-site blogging therefore helps you to optimize your business's visibility in the search engines.

This is important for two reasons:

- When a client uses those keywords to search for editing and proofreading services, you're more likely to be found. In other words, your blog is working for your business by making it discoverable ... entry through a back door, if you like.
- Even if a client isn't yet ready to commission editorial services, they might be in the future. If they're using Google to search for solutions to self-editing or writing problems, the keyword juice in your blog posts can pull them in. Then, when they're ready to source an editor, you'll be top of mind because you've instilled trust with your problem-solving (see 'Holism', above).

Creating second homes – libraries and hubs

If people don't know you, they don't search online for your blog. They search online for *solutions*. If they click through to our websites, via a directory for example, the first place they'll head for is unlikely to be the blog tab. And even if is, will our visitor find the answer to their problems in the content that's visible on the first page of the blog? If we only have 10 pieces of content, yes. What if we have 40? How about 500?

The solution is to create second homes for our blog content – libraries, hubs, resource centres ... call them what you will.

I'd love to have a second home – a nice holiday cottage somewhere pleasant. Alas, the coffers won't stretch to it! If only I could somehow feed my current home through some sort of time–space warp and plonk myself somewhere warm and sunny without wrecking my current home. And all for no money, of course!

Those lucky blogs – they get to have all the fun. Because that's exactly what they can do! All you need is a new page where you'll create your library or hub. How you design it is up to you. One option is to create a bank of images or colour blocks with text that tells your visitors what's on offer. Then link the images to the relevant posts on your blog.

How content libraries aid navigation

Blogs can be tricky to navigate. It's one thing to hold someone's interest when they've searched for one solution and found it. But what happens when they're done? If you blog regularly you'll build a bank of articles that might also be relevant to your visitor.

If your visitor is already interested in exploring an archive on a subject of particular interest, all well and good. Blog archives are essential for this reason. However, they're tricky to customize. With some website hosts (Weebly, for example) the content tends to be listed chronologically, which means that older relevant content might be too far down the list to catch a busy visitor's eye.

A search tool can help, though that assumes your visitor is ready and willing to invest the time.

What you need is a library, a digital room in which your visitors can browse your very best content ... an inviting space into which your blog content feeds.

It's worth thinking about how twenty-first century users consume content. It's not uncommon for any of us to binge – whether we're watching, listening or reading. That makes sense in the business sphere, too, because we're all busy and easily distracted. And so the easier we can make it for our clients to find our great stuff, the more likely we are to remain top of mind.

And that's where libraries or content hubs come into their own. They allow us to take our blog content and make it visible in a space that we control. And not just our blog articles. We can use the hub to house complementary videos, booklets and checklists (some of which we'll have repurposed from our blog articles) too.

Case study: The content library

The content library on my website includes the following:

- Videos embedded from my YouTube channel
- Podcasts I've guested on
- Booklets
- Thumbnail images that link to individual relevant blog posts

You might also include a message of intention so that visitors know what they're looking at, and an invitation to sign up to your blog. If you have a separate mailing list or newsletter for potential clients, feature that on your hub page instead.

Note that none of this content is fresh – all of it feeds in from somewhere else on my website or a third-party site. The only additional effort I made was to create the page, upload the images and add in the links.

This library is one of the most visited page on my website after the blog. It's completely client-focused – dedicated to solving authors' problems – and its aim is to make me look like a superhero. And instead of waiting for visitors to decide what they might like to search for, I show them what else is on offer.

For you to do ...

Think about where your blog lives. Bear in mind the following:

- The holistic message you want to convey.
- The proximity of your services and your content.
- How the search engines work.

Then consider how accessible that content is elsewhere on your site.

- What happens when a potential client lands on other pages?

- Does your website make them feel as if you're a superhero editor?
- Can they browse through your very best stuff, regardless of when it was published?

Make a note of any changes you need to make in terms of where your blog lives. Sketch out the architecture of your resource hub. Think about:

- The blog content you'll include
- Images
- Colour blocks
- Text
- Links
- Related resources such as videos, guest posts, booklets, tip sheets and checklists
- A message of intention to your target audience
- Invitations and calls to action for a newsletter, mailing list or blog sign-up

5. Blog design and structure

Overview

Your blog design and structure will be determined in part by your host. Weebly's options are less sophisticated than some of the Wordpress templates I've seen, many of which offer attractive and easily accessible buckets of content. All of us have to work with what we've got.

Even if your host offers a basic layout, you can still make it sing by being creative with banner images. Ultimately, it's the content that counts. You could have the flashiest theme on the planet but if your content is boring your blog won't help you grow your business.

Design and structure are important because it matters little how great your headers are or how many rich keywords you include, or how well you've set up your metadata if when your visitors arrive on your blog they're bored rigid. They'll leave as fast as they came and they won't share, talk about, link to, recommend your blog content. You'll be instantly forgettable.

Blog page – what to include

Here are some ideas to consider when designing your blog. Again, what you'll opt for will be determined in part by what's available from your host.

Give the blog a name

Give your blog an identity! It brings vitality to it, and over time can become part of your brand identity. Just as a name can help us to remember and refer to a person, so it can with our content. Some of my colleagues don't know the type of editorial services I specialize in but they know the name of my blog!

Think about what your blog will be about, what you're trying to do with it, and whom it's aimed at. That will give you ideas for names. If the name of your blog includes a relevant keyword that could give you an SEO bump, all the better.

Here are some examples from the international editorial community:

- Clarity (Lisa Poisso)
- Eat Sleep Edit Repeat (Liz Jones)

- Sentence First (Stan Carey)
- The Editing Essentials Blog (Denise Cowle)
- The Editing Blog (Louise Harnby)

Most editors and proofreaders are not naming their blogs so it's yet another way to differentiate your content.

Utilize the sidebar

If your theme allows for it, use your sidebar creatively. Most website hosts allow for the basics such as monthly archives and categories. Consider introducing some of these extras:

- **A search tool:** I think these are key. If someone's landed on your blog and they're ready to delve, they'll need something to help them. No one will bother scrolling through more than a couple of pages in an archive, even if they're really interested. And if some of great content is old, it'll be missed. Search boxes make life easier for the reader who's raised their hand and said, 'I'm interested in what you're doing, but I haven't got all day!'
- **Linked images:** If you've written or contributed to a book, created an outstanding free resource, offer specialist training, or offer complementary services such as speaking, advertise it in the sidebar and create links to any relevant internal pages in your website.
- **A headshot:** Including an image of yourself reminds readers that the blog's written by a human being. The image helps to link your content to your services by making the blog recognizable. I decided to include a fun one, though it was taken during the same shoot as my regular headshots so there's brand consistency.
- **Award or membership badges:** Are you a member of a professional editorial society? Have you been nominated for or won an award that's relevant to your industry or your clients' industries? Have you been featured on or contributed to a relevant and well-known blog? Tell people about it in the sidebar.
- **A copyright-protection message:** Include a copyright statement that requests people to seek permission before copying your content. Copyscape offers free badges that you can embed in your blog sidebar.

- **High-performing or recent content:** Include links to your popular content, regardless of how old it is. Check what's working using an analytics tool. Or feature recent posts that you want to promote.
- **Links to recent comments:** Draw readers' attention to top-performing posts by listing recent comments (if your host allows for it).
- **Sharing buttons:** If you haven't installed sharing buttons on each page of your website, include them in the sidebar as well in individual blog posts. Make it as easy as possible for readers to share with your content. I recommend Shareaholic because it works with most websites and can be customized to match your brand colours.
- **Sign-up button:** Help your readers to stay in touch by including a sign-up or subscription button. I recommend MailChimp to host your subscriber list. It's free for up to 2,000 subs.

Blog banner

If your website host allows for it, consider including a banner that identifies your blog. This is especially useful if you've given your blog a name. Plus, you're giving your readers an important message – that they're in a specific place with a specific type of content that's not just some add-on. It's a serious space with an identity ... a purposeful home for useful, valuable stuff that you're committed to writing regularly.

You could either follow the design of your existing pages, or create a custom banner that's related to your blog's name. Think about your colour way so that you stay on brand.

Most of the examples I found of banner images were those on blogs that existed as separate entities from the editors' primary business websites, so if you can add a banner image onto your business site-based blog, it's yet another opportunity to stand out.

Individual posts – what to include

Now let's consider the individual post elements.

Headlines

'Your headline is the thing that is going to persuade people to click through your blog post. Fail with your headline and no one is going to read,' says pro blogger Amanda Webb.

When it comes to the search engines, your lovely headshots, informational images and fabulously helpful body text won't be working for you. It's headlines that show up.

Headlines are important for two reasons:

- **Mechanics** – the search-engine algorithms choose what ranks where
- **Emotions** – humans choose whether to click through

So an SEO-rich headline might get you high up in Google's search rankings but it could still be so dull as to leave a potential client wondering why on earth they should bother. Great headlines therefore need to work on a mechanical and emotional level.

And it's not just visitors, it's the right visitors ... those who are going to link to, like, share, discuss, and recommend your blog content, and those who are going to buy from us.

The mechanics behind rankability

I like CoSchedule's free Headline Analyzer. CoSchedule recommends creating headlines that satisfy the following criteria:

- Incorporate questions, how-tos and lists
- Have a balance of common and uncommon words
- Include emotional words
- Are long enough to inform but short enough to scan and digest

Paste your headline into the tool and CoShedule will analyse it, give you a score, and tell you where the potential problems are.

The emotion behind clickability

I use the Emotional Marketing Value Headline Analyzer. That's because, SEO rankings aside, it's human beings who decide what to do next. This tool is therefore useful when we're sharing our posts on social media and if people are already on our blog and wondering whether to continue reading.

This tool limits your headline to 20 words and measures the potential impact of those words based on the following:

- Intellectualism
- Empathy
- Spirituality

I think it's a great tool for our community because we're so often handling text that's personal to our clients. It requires a high degree of trust to hand over written work and pay to have it edited by someone who's more than likely a stranger. This tool allows us to evaluate our headlines in a way that respects that.

Regardless of the post's final title on the blog page, create a couple of extra titles for social media sharing. That way you can keep things fresh rather than inducing audience fatigue. This is important when promoting our blog content because great content shouldn't be posted just once; we need to place it into a rotation schedule.

Body-text design

Let's consider the text, since that's the meat of the post and where the true value lies for your reader. Making that accessible will help with the shares, likes, comments and links that will put you and your business top of the search engines and top of mind.

Paragraph length

Paragraphs should be short, just two or three sentences. This can be a tricky concept for editors to get their heads around because we're used to dealing with media in which it's conventional to create paragraphs based on theme or topic. In the blogging world, readers' attention spans are shorter; appearance trumps coherence. That means that you might be introducing paragraphs breaks where they're not needed according to publishing convention.

Mobile-user experience

It's essential that editor bloggers consider the mobile-user experience when creating content. Longer paragraphs appear as unwieldy walls of text on a smart phone. We're trying to engage readers not put them off, so think beyond the large screen and respect the fact that your readers will be accessing your content on different devices. Go to Google Analytics, select Audience, Mobile, and Overview. That will show you how your users are accessing your content.

Easy reading

Text should be scannable and digestible. In addition to text blocks, use bulleted lists and headings to help your readers access the key messages in your posts fast.

Introductory paragraph

Pay attention to your introductory paragraph. Pro marketers Andrew and Pete advised me that this is important because it's what Google will pull from the blog for its short description.

Blog-post length

Consider the length of your post. 'Google is a research tool. Longer pages have more opportunities to indicate their relevance. Google sees longer pages as more likely to contain the answer to the searcher's question,' says Andy Crestodina ('The Ideal Length for Blog Posts, Tweets, and Everything Else in Your Marketing'). To maximize search-engine traffic, aim for around 1,500 words of high-quality, relevant content.

Don't be a slave to the numbers though. If you can solve someone's problem in 250 words, that's what you should do. It's not all about Google. If Professor X lands on your blog and has to wade through 1,500 words to find a solution that you could have expressed in 200, she'll get bored and leave. And she won't share, like, comment on or bookmark your blog post. Nor will she hire you if the editors she likes working with are those who can help her remove the waffle from her work. Quality trumps quantity every time.

Call to action

Include a call to action. I'm terrible at remembering to do this! However, the experts say that we should always round off our blog posts with a clear call to action: Ask a question, tell the reader how they can share, encourage a comment, or tell them how to sign-up to your subscriber list. People are much more likely to do something if you ask them to.

Images

Break up boring walls of text with images, videos and gifs.

- **Informational images** nudge the reader by showing them what they're in for – why they should bother investing time in digesting 1,500 words. And you can use them on social media to make your posts stand out, especially on Twitter, where the eye is assaulted by a stream of fast-moving text.

- Add **alt-text** to your images when you upload them to your blog. The search engines like it and it respects the visually impaired.
- Break up walls of text with images that tell the reader **what's coming** in the following paragraphs. Or insert **infographics** to make your blog content more digestible.
- Images are perfect for styling a **series**. That's important because if readers find one post in a series and like it, they're more likely to click through to find the sister posts. If you've not told them your great content is part of a family they won't think to look.
- **Video** offers readers an alternative way of accessing your blog content and can be repurposed on social media and hosted on your YouTube channel. Plus, people are curious, and piquing curiosity keeps visitors on your site for longer. That's something else the search engines like because it tells them you're providing a quality user experience. Your videos needn't be long ... just short introductions to your blog that tell the reader the key points you'll cover. Furthermore, you show your audience the real you, which increases trust.
- **Gifs** are teeny-weeny videos – a collection of images on steroids! They're a fun and alternative way to evoke emotion and make your blog posts memorable, and you can repurpose them for social media. You can use digital photographs, stills from your videos, or create images in Canva. Once you have your images, upload the media to a gif creator. I recommend Gifmaker.me and Giphy. There's an example of a gif I created for a guest blog post from Andrew and Pete on video marketing at 'Why video marketing is important for proofreaders too'.

Internal linking

Internal links are good for SEO because they tell the search engines that your site is full of relevant content. Consider the following:

- Include your **bio** at the end of each article. See the previous section on introductory paragraphs and how Google includes some of my bio in its short descriptions. I love what it's including because it tells readers what I do as an editor rather than as a blogger. It's also a great way of including internal links to your products, services and content libraries (see 'Creating Second Homes').

- Create a **list of related articles**. It gives you an SEO boost and helps your readers navigate your blog by pointing them in the direction of content they'd otherwise be unaware of. Plus, you'll increase your authority by showing them that you're not just a one-trick pony. Your content log will help you to access related content quickly, particularly once you've built up a large archive of posts.

Enable sharing

Make it as easy as possible for your advocate colleagues and potential clients to share your valuable blog content.

Include sharing buttons in every blog post. I put mine at the bottom under my bio and near the top of each post because some busy readers will share without reading our content in full. I recommend Shareaholic because you can customize them with your brand colours.

I'm still surprised by how many editors don't include sharing buttons on their individual blog articles. It means I have to copy the link, open up the social media platform, create the share, tag the author, and post. If your reader is pushed for time they might decide not to bother. That's a missed opportunity.

The click-to-tweet tool is a nice feature that enables you to ask for specific quotes from your blog posts to be shared. I've been slack about using this. You don't need to be!

You can embed tweets and LinkedIn content in your blog articles to add interest with just a few clicks. For tweets, click the chevron in the top-right corner of a tweet, select Embed tweet, then copy the code and paste it into your blog post using your embed-code tool. For LinkedIn, click the ellipsis in the top-right corner of a post, select Embed this post, then Copy code. Again, paste the code into your blog post using the embed-code tool.

Commenting, sign-up and metadata

Make it easy for you audience to engage – now and in the future.

- Enable commenting. Make sure you respond to everyone who takes the time to chip in.
- Include a blog sign-up/subscription button.

- Most blogs allow you to input some metadata for the search engines and the sidebar information – short description, title, permalink, categories, commenting, scheduling date, keywords, and so on. Your platform will determine what's on offer. Do remember to fill this in. I figure that if it's there, it's there for a reason, so use it!

For you to do ...

Record your ideas about the following:

- Blog name
- Sidebar information
- Banner imagery
- Internal images
- The tools and plugins you'll be using for headlines, sharing and subscription management

6. Blog promotion

Overview

If no one knows your blog exists, how can they share, like, comment on, and talk about your content, you and your business? Blogging without blog promotion is a supreme waste of time. We could spend hours crafting beautiful content for our target audience, but if we don't make it visible it will have no purposeful business or economic value.

Crafting promotion for social media

Whatever your preferred tactics for blog promotion, one thing's for sure: social media is the promo superhero. The three biggest platforms – LinkedIn, Twitter and Facebook – offer a superb suite of tools to help us get out there. Ultimately, your chosen platforms should be those which your advocate colleagues and potential clients are using.

When we use social media as part of our content-marketing strategy we get eyes on our blog posts. And the more people who see them, the more likely we are to receive likes, shares, comments and engagement – all of which helps to make us visible in the search engines and top of our colleagues' and clients' minds.

It's about more than just posting links and pretty pictures, now so more than ever. We must work increasingly hard on these busy platforms with their ever-shifting algorithms. However, persistence pays and there's no faster way to get your blog content, and your business, in front of people than by embracing social media.

By automating the scheduling of our evergreen posts, time is freed up for posting manually onto our core platforms; manual posting allows us to craft our promotional posts with the algorithms in mind.

Consider the following:

- Uploading blog posts natively (direct to the platform) rather than linking.
- Creating mini summaries of a blog post on a Page that invite conversations.
- Uploading sharable videos that summarize the core themes of a post.

- Running chatbot campaigns that include booklets repurposed from blog content.
- Uploading vlog versions of blog content.
- Going live with a summary of your content.
- Posting links to blog posts in groups if that content answers a specific question.
- Joining blog linky parties in Facebook groups where the practice is encouraged.

More promotion ideas

Here are some additional ideas to consider for blog promotion:

Colleague love

Encourage your colleagues to share by including them in your blog posts and tagging them when you share that content.

Email blog posts to subscribers

Use your subscription list to automatically deliver your posts to your subscribers. Subscribers have told you they want to receive emails alerts from you so don't be shy about doing this regularly.

Include discoverable keywords

Keywords help blog promotion because they make you findable in the search engines. Don't overthink this or deliberately keyword-stuff your posts – if you're writing targeted content for a specific audience and you're solving their problems, you'll likely use the very keywords that will make your content discoverable. If you're not including the right keywords, you're probably not creating the right kind of content.

Double up your share buttons

Place share buttons at the top and bottom of your blog post. This not only makes it ultra-easy for your fans to share your articles, but also looks great if you have a popular post with lots of shares.

Directory entries

If the platform allows it, link to your blog (or your blog's second home) via your key advertising directories. Directories will force you to communicate your offering using a fixed layout but by linking to your valuable content you can move potential clients off that site and onto your own.

Carnival of the Indies

If you've written a blog post that's relevant to indie authors and self-publishers, submit it for inclusion in Joel Friedlander's monthly Carnival of the Indies. If your submission is accepted, you'll generate more traffic to the original post on your website for little additional effort. Friedlander promotes the Carnival on Twitter to his 44.3K followers. That's a lot of potential eyes on your blog post!

Include a free resource or download

By adding a tip sheet, booklet or some other resource, you'll add value to your blog post. Some people choose to make these available only in exchange for an email address. Marketers call this 'gating' the content because we're putting it behind a gate that's only unlocked in exchange for something in return. The gated content is called a 'lead magnet' because it's attractive enough to make subscribers think it's worth handing over their data for.

This can be a useful tactic if you want to build your email subscription list and actively sell to people via email.

Create and use a Pinterest board

Pinterest isn't a big platform for me but it's simple and quick to create a board and to pin images of blog content to it.

Promote older blogs in your current content

If you have several blog posts related to your most recent one, include links to them in a Related Reading section at the end of that post. That makes sense because if someone's currently reading your article on, for example, narrative point of view, they have their hands raised for related story-craft content but might not know that it exists on your blog. By linking, you show them the way.

There's another benefit – you're creating high-quality, relevant internal links within your own website. That's a signal to the search engines that you're helping your visitor to navigate the space.

Work with others outside your field

Don't be afraid to step out of your bubble. I've invited guests onto my blog (and provided content for them) who work outside the editorial and community. I've also done a podcast interviews on Tim Lewis's Begin Self-Publishing Podcast, Natalie Hailey's Hot Content Podcast, Roger Edwards's Marketing and Finance Podcast, and I've written for marketers Andrew and Pete.

Because those professionals work in other communities, they put me, my website and my blog content in front of new audiences. And it can lead to work leads because, after all, lots of people need editors!

Include 'click to tweets'

This encourages your readers to share your chosen key quotes or images from posts. Writer Jake Poinier (Dr Freelance) utilizes this tool often, and it's one of way of ensuring that retweets are kept fresh because readers can select different options.

Re-share relevant content

Don't make the mistake of thinking you need only promote a blog post once. Reschedule your content frequently so that those who missed it the first time around have another opportunity. The more times you get a blog post out there, the fewer likes and comments it will get, but it's not always about the numbers.

You're also reminding people that you have a bank of blogs, that you post regularly, and that you're engaged with the issues that your community and clients have concerns about. See 'The Schedule and the Scheduler' section for more detail.

Make old posts look new

You can take an old post and freshen it up by repurposing the content in some way. Use a tool like MoShow or Lumen5.

Add invitations to your second homes

If you've set up a second home (content library/resource page) as I hope you have – or will – remember to promote your blog there, preferably with a subscription button.

Use your social media profiles

Place links to the blog in your social media profiles. Twitter offers the most visible option, but you can include it in the Story notes on your Facebook page too.

To complicate things, your Facebook profile also has a section called Notes. This is not to be confused with the Facebook **page** native-blogging platform called Notes. In the **profile** Notes section you can add information and links to core resources: I've included my blog and my proofreading stamps. Access the profile Notes tool via the More tab on your profile.

On LinkedIn you can upload links to various media. Select the Me tab from the LinkedIn ribbon. Underneath your banner picture, click on the pen icon. Scroll down the Media section and click on the Link button. Now you can add your blog URL (and other resource pages).

Awards

If a friend nominates you for a blog award (or any award for that matter) great! Some awards programmes allow you to enter yourself. Don't be shy. You have to be in it to win it, or so they say. And it really isn't about the winning but about making your business visible to potential clients.

Ireland, the UK and South Africa all have annual blogging awards – why not see whether your blog might fit into any of their categories?

For you to do ...

Think about the promotional opportunities on your own website:

- Reread the section on building second homes. Your content library is the perfect promotional tool for your content because it's easier to find and navigate. Make the most of it!
- Use each blog post to promote older but related posts.
- Recycle posts into lead magnets and resources that you can use as downloadable giveaways.

Consider external resources through which you can tell people about your blog articles:

- Directories
- Blog carnivals, roundups and linky parties

And focus on social media:

- Automating scheduled promotion of evergreen content
- Crafting algorithm-friendly posts on your primary platforms

7. Keeping a content log

Overview

I recommend you create a content log. The idea came from my marketing coaches back in 2017 and it's saved me oodles of time. It's nothing fancy – just a spreadsheet that records the following:

- Title of blog or vlog (including guest posts from colleagues, and my guest content on their sites)
- Date published
- URL
- Subject or topic
- Any further action to be taken
- Additional notes
- Days of the month on which I'll promote content old and new

I also record ideas about future blogs (and complementary vlogs) just in case I forget.

Why do we need a content log?

Content logs save us time because once we begin to build an archive of blog posts – and other materials – it's easy to forget what we have. By recording what we've created, we provide ourselves with a one-stop shop that lets us access that content efficiently. Efficient access is useful in the following scenarios:

- Responding to questions
- Repurposing and recycling
- Collation for internal link juice
- Recording a social media schedule

Responding to questions

Imagine a colleague or client asks you a question. You've already addressed the topic three times on the blog, each time approaching it from a different angle, and you've created a video tutorial on YouTube.

You could write a long email but that would entail repeating what you've already written. The alternative is to search for each related blog post (perhaps via your Search tool), copy and paste the title into your email, then do the same with each URL. Plus, you'd have to repeat the process for the video in YouTube. It's a tad laborious, and you're busy.

With a content log, you can focus on topic. So if the question falls under the umbrella of academic style, you can sort your log on this subject, drag your cursor over the relevant group of titles and URLs, and copy and paste the cells into your email.

Even if you're just looking for one specific post, it's quicker to search by keyword in Excel, and copy and paste the title and URL, than it is to access the information via your blog or vlog. And because you're logging all your content, regardless of the platform on which it's published, you can direct the questioner to relevant articles on more than one platform (even guest articles).

Repurposing and recycling

The content log is the perfect tool to help us repurpose and recycle, particularly once we've developed an extensive bank of content. My editorial blog was born in 2011 so I have hundreds of articles in my archive. I forget what I published a year ago never mind seven! My log allows me to browse the titles and remind myself of what's there and quickly click through.

What I find doesn't always please me! Not all of those articles are great, I'll admit. Blogging, like anything, is a journey of learning and growth. Some of my content could do with an overhaul. So what's wrong with it?

- Some articles are just out of date; either I've moved on or the world has – they need to be recycled in the form of fresh posts.
- Some could be better written even though I'm happy with the material – they need to be edited.
- Some are fine in terms of content but the layout and branding are poor – they need a new wardrobe!

And then there's the content that I'm happy with but that offers a back door into fresh content with little additional effort. This fall into two categories:

- Articles that are not on my own site – they need to be rebuilt in a way that allows me to bring them home.

- Articles such as related or series posts that are ripe for collation into new formats that some of my readers might find more convenient – they need repurposed as ebooklets.

Collation for internal link juice

It's good practice to include a list of related posts at the end of each blog article. I must confess to forgetting to do this frequently myself, so don't follow my lead! The search engines like to see relevant links on our website pages – it demonstrates relevance and authority. Linking to our own pages internally therefore helps with our SEO.

By sorting via the subject column, or doing keyword searches in our content log, we can grab and collate the relevant posts quickly.

Recording a social media schedule

Social media platforms are constantly shifting their algorithms and changing their policies about what is and what is not acceptable. In March 2018 full automation via schedulers died, on Twitter at least. Twitter announced that, in a bid to reduce spam, the same tweet could not be posted from multiple Twitter accounts.

I'd previously used (and recommended) auto-schedulers such as Recurpost and Buffer. Recurpost was fantastic for Twitter because we could upload a short piece of text, a supporting image, and a link to a blog post once and once only. We set the days of the month on which we wanted the tweet to be published and then forgot about it. Everything was done for us. It was amazing for delivering evergreen content on a regular basis.

When Twitter changed its policy, Recurpost introduced strict auto-scheduling policies. It would no longer allow us to recycle the same tweet over and over. Instead, we'd have to create manual alternative texts in bulk. Recurpost would select a text, use it one time, and move on to the next text when it was scheduled to tweet the link to our blog posts. When it ran out of alternatives, it would stop posting for us. And at that point, Recurpost lost its usefulness.

Why? Because if we have a blog post that we want to tweet about twice a month, we'd have to create 24 lines of text just to ensure that once post would be scheduled unproblematically for a year. If we have 50 blog posts, it becomes untenable for the sole trader who has to do everything themselves.

Will other social media platforms change their policies on auto-scheduling? Possibly. Probably. So it's back to basics. It means a little more graft for us but there's a tool that can help us: the content log.

The content log is the perfect place to record which days of the month you are going to post your blog content – your recent stuff and your older posts.

Open your log every day. Use the Find tool in Excel to search for the day number. Then use the links provided to share the appropriate posts on social media. Just remember to create fresh text every time so that the tweets look original.

For you to do ...

Create a content-log Excel template. If you already have blog articles published, record them in your spreadsheet straightaway so that you get yourself into the mindset of regularly filling in your log.

You might find it useful to add in the days of the month when you'll share a post on social media.

8. Scheduling your blog posts

Overview

When we're blogging we need to decide on the following:

- How often we're going to publish
- What tools we'll use to deliver our content so that it's visible

We need a schedule and a scheduler.

How to approach the schedule

How often should you publish?

Regularly and consistently is the short answer. Given that we're not just creating content for the heck of it, but to generate visibility and leads, there are four factors that the editorial blogger needs to be aware of:

- The search engines' preferences
- Readers' perceptions and building trust
- The impact of multiple points of entry to your website
- The kick-in time for visibility

Search-engine preferences

The search-engine algorithms love fresh content because it indicates that a website is active and dedicated to providing a good user experience.

Blogging regularly is a shortcut to freshness. The more frequently you do it, the more often the spiders crawling over your website find new stuff. Over time, you'll be rewarded with higher rankings for keywords, which means more visitors to your site and more potential clients asking you for quotes.

Readers' perceptions and building trust

We have to earn the right to be top of mind for referrals and benefit from our colleagues' and clients' SEO-driving activity.

This is how a reader perceives a blog that publishes content irregularly:

- The blogger doesn't know their stuff well enough to solve problems
- The blogger isn't committed or can't be bothered to solve problems

Those feelings don't inspire trust. If your window cleaner couldn't be bothered to clean your windows on a regular basis, how quickly would you try to find a replacement? It's the same with blogging. No one's going to talk about or share our content if we can't be bothered to create it regularly.

If you publish to a regular schedule, people get used to seeing your blog posts. And having earned that trust, it's essential to maintain it. Nothing will trash it faster than three months of bloggy brilliance followed by silence because you ran out of gas.

Do a great job consistently and your readers are more likely to subscribe. And that means a higher chance of comments, shares, likes, and recommendations. Mess them around and they'll lose interest. The online world is a fast-moving one and you're operating in a global market. If a reader can't get the answers from you, they'll switch their allegiances to someone who will. Plus, commitment tells your audience something about you as an editorial business owner – that you don't mess around, that when you embark on a project you stick with it.

The impact of multiple points of entry to your website

Publish one great blog post about fiction editing and you have one point of entry in the search engines and in the list of resources that might be referred to by your colleagues in a forum.

What does that mean a year down the line if you publish every two weeks? Now you have 26 points of entry. That's 26 opportunities to be found, to be visible ... 26 ways in which a potential client might end up on your website.

The kick-in time for visibility

The more regularly you blog, the quicker you'll see the benefits for your business. There's no magic number. 'Publish this number of blog posts and the world will be your oyster' – that's not what's going on here. However, what research, and my own experience, has shown is that it can take around two years to see the impact of a sound marketing plan. But that two years has to be an *active* two years. I blogged around every two weeks when I began my journey and it took me 24 months to see the impact in the search engines. That's 52 articles.

I'm not promising that by blogging weekly you'll be able to throw your hat in the air after 12 months because you're booked up so far in advance that you turn away more work than you accept. There are too many other factors to consider, such as whether that content is being delivered to the right audience via the right platforms and in a format they want. What I am saying is that the more active you are, the faster you'll see results.

Mindfulness – build-up versus burn-out

Be mindful of what's achievable on a personal level. Blogging weekly doesn't wear me out; I find it therapeutic. But you and I might be two different animals with different lives, different demands, different goals. What works for me might not work for you. You should choose a publishing schedule that fits *your* business goals and *your* personality, and stick to that, whether it be twice weekly or twice monthly.

We should always aim for quality, too, because that trumps everything. If you publish weekly but your posts don't engage – no shares, no likes, no comments – your blog won't be sticky, won't compel people to work with you or to refer others to you.

The scheduler

Manual delivery of blog content is time-consuming. Marketing is important, but not if it impinges drastically on our editing and leisure time.

An auto-scheduler helps us automate the process to a degree by posting one piece of content over several different social media platforms at the same time. There are lots to choose from: SmarterQueue, Buffer, Hootsuite, FollowingLike, Amlifr, SocialPilot, Recurpost, KUKU, Jarvis. Some are free, others have premium versions with higher functionality. Some monitor what your network's up to, though the consequence is a more crowded dashboard.

However, take care with set-and-forget auto-scheduling because of the Twitter spam policy. You can still use schedulers but you'll need to put in some manual work to ensure the text is always varied. I use Buffer in conjunction with my content log.

Reposting blog content on social media

To maximize engagement, you should be posting regularly so that you build a reputation as an editorial professional who is consistently engaged.

So how often should you reschedule content? It depends on the platform, where your audience is hanging out, and what's performing well.

Consider the noise levels and pace – the greater the traffic levels and the higher the speed at which posts appear, the more likely your post is to be buried and the more you can reschedule without frustrating your audience.

Evaluating

My two preferred analytics tools are **Google Analytics** and **StatCounter**. Both provide a broad picture of what people are looking at on our websites, and they show us the type of content that's getting the most attention – what our audience finds most useful. That helps us decide what we should create more of and what we should be reposting.

These tools are brilliant at helping us make decisions that are based on *data* rather than *instinct*.

You might also decide to dig a little deeper with Google Analytics by creating 'goals'. I've set up goals that show me which social media platforms are driving the most traffic to my blog over a given time period.

I recommend Andy Crestodina's blog at Orbit Media for straightforward advice on how to get the most from Google Analytics.

For you to do ...

Decide on the following:

- How often will you publish blog posts? Think about the amount of time you can build into your working week to research, write, edit and publish your quality articles.
- Be mindful – make a list of any potential stress points that could impact on your publication schedule. It's better to build up than burn out.
- Use your content log to create a schedule of what will be shared and when.
- Make a note on the analytics software you'll install to help you evaluate which blog posts are performing well and how readers are finding them.
- Set up goals in Google Analytics so that your data is answering your questions.

9. Subscription

Overview

Build a subscription list via your blog. When someone bothers to subscribe, they're raising their hand and saying, 'I'm interested in you and what you're saying.' This means they're more likely to read, share, like, link to and recommend your posts to other people in their communities. They're also more likely to buy from you.

MailChimp

For new bloggers, I recommend MailChimp:

Cost

As far as I'm aware, it's the only pro email marketing platform that's free ... to a point. Once you reach the 2,000 threshold it will cost you, but if you're at the beginning of your blogging journey it will serve you perfectly well for a number of years.

The free plan entitles you to send up to 12,000 emails per month. So if you have a subscriber list of 600, you could deliver 20 blog posts.

ConvertKit and FloDesk are two paid-for options that are well regarded.

Customization

MailChimp has a set of tools that allow you to customize the layout of your emails. Plus, you can capture certain types of information to help you understand who your subscribers are. For example, I ask subscribers to tell me whether they're a writer or an editor.

If you plan to use your subscription list to mail information other than your blog posts, make it clear at sign-up stage so that your subscribers know what to expect.

Double opt-in

Mailchimp includes a double opt-in so your list is compliant with the General Data Protection Regulation. That means someone must input their email address to subscribe, and confirm via email that they'd like to go ahead. That's important because there are hefty fines for organizations of any size found to be in contravention of the GDPR.

For you to do ...

Now do the following:

- Decide which tool you'll use to collect and store your subscribers.
- Set up automatic blog delivery.
- Ensure your subscription form includes a double opt-in so that you're GDPR-compliant.
- Sketch out some ideas about how you'll use your subscription list – to deliver just your blog content or to mail other information or offers.

10. Measuring success

Overview

Having put so much work into building a blog, we need to know that it's taking us forward. Success – however we define it – won't happen overnight. For that reason we need to start tracking early.

There are different ways of measuring success. When it comes to blogging, the baselines are about engagement, relationships and visibility. The end point is ideal clients who'll pay our price. With that in mind, here's what you might look at.

Direct metrics

As you build your blog, keep track of key metrics that give you information about the health of your business.

Page views

Track the total page-view data on your blog as a whole and for specific articles. You'll discover which content is most interesting to your audience over time; you'll also feel encouraged by the fact that people are visiting your blog.

Google Analytics is the best free tool for the job in my opinion. To the uninitiated it can feel somewhat daunting but it's worth persevering because it provides us with a range of useful insights that help us make decisions and encourage us to keep going. StatCounter is a great secondary backup.

Goals achieved

Google Analytics allows you to set up goals so that you can see how visitors flow from social media or the search engines to specific pages on your site that are key to business growth (e.g. contact pages, sales pages, second homes aimed at clients).

Comments on social media

The more comments you receive on social media, the more the algorithms will reward you by prioritizing your post and pushing it out to a wider audience (organic reach). The numbers aside, commenting requires effort and shows that people are interested in what you're doing with your blog. Those people are more likely to subscribe, and to recommend and share your articles. That, in turn, has SEO benefits.

On your Facebook business page, check Insights.

In Twitter, check Analytics (from the dropdown menu after you've clicked on your profile picture).

In LinkedIn, keep an eye on the views per post (profile picture in ribbon > Me > Posts and Activity).

Comments on your blog

Are people bothering to comment on your blog posts? If so, well done. It requires effort to bother commenting and demonstrates a desire to engage with you. Again, those people are more likely to subscribe, and to recommend and share your articles. That, in turn, has SEO benefits.

Conversations

Are people talking to you about your articles – either via email, on social media, by phone, via Messenger? If they are, it proves you're increasing engagement and building relationships. If you're struggling, consider whether you can promote your blog content in ways that encourage conversations.

Downloads of our content

StatCounter provides data on downloads (if you've uploaded files to your blog). However, the data for the free log is limited so you won't be able to access numbers for all time. Still, it's another metric for audience engagement so worth paying attention to even if it's just a partial snapshot.

Referrals to your articles

Google Analytics also holds metrics on referrals to your content from other websites. Select your date range, choose Acquisitions, then Overview, and you'll see how many referrals you're getting. Click on Referrals to see exactly which sites people are clicking through from.

Requests to advertise on your blog

These are almost always irrelevant to the blog's audience and content! Whether you choose to accept them (and monetize your blog) or not is a personal choice. I choose not to accept them, but it's nice to be asked. If you decide to decline, be polite so that you can change your mind! And recognize that you've been asked because the advertiser believes they can generate revenue by being visible on your blog. That's a positive insight to how you're perceived in the world beyond your community.

Requests to guest post on your blog

Unless guest blogging arises out of a discussion with a colleague (usually about mutual guesting), these tend to be from content writers looking for quick backlinks rather than people who are interested in providing substantive problem-solving content that's relevant to your blog. I don't accept such requests but receiving them pleases me because it's a reminder that my blog is visible and that my blog has authority within the search engines.

Search-engine rankings

Do incognito searches for keyword terms that you want to be found for. Don't fret if you're not on page one after you've published ten blog posts. It's going to take a lot more than that! StatCounter generates some useful reports that show you a range of Google pages on which you rank for keywords. The data is not complete by any stretch (most of the keyword terms for which I've been found are hidden) but it gives you a glimpse.

Shares on social media

If you're rescheduling older content, you're likely to get fewer shares because your core audience will have already seen the posts. Shares, likes and retweets on social for fresh content are likely to be higher and drive direct traffic to your site. It's worth watching this data because it shows you what topics people want to engage with.

Subscription sign-ups

Keep an eye on your blog-subscriber numbers. You don't need to be slavish about it but it will give you a huge sense of satisfaction when you see your audience increasing. These are people who've made the effort to raise their hands and say, 'I don't want to miss a thing you write.'

Indirect metrics

It's difficult to attribute some insights directly to your blogging work but correlations are easier if you dig into the data at regular intervals and set it alongside your blogging activity.

Emails in which colleagues or clients praise your site:

Keep a note of when people tell you how much value you've offered on your website. This is where your second homes can work really hard for you because they evoke positive emotion in the people whose problems you've solved.

Enquiry rates

Track the number of enquiries you get, and where they came from. I use an Excel spreadsheet on my phone and now have several years' worth of data.

Income for hours worked

Track your earnings on a job-by-job basis, and how many hours you've worked. Then evaluate quarterly and annually. Over time you'll get a sense of whether you're earning more, or the same but for fewer hours. Set this data against your direct metrics to garner insights about the impact of your blogging activity on paid work.

Quality of the clients and work offers

Record any changes you notice in the type of quotes being requested and the offers of work. As you gain traction in the search engines, and drive more traffic to your site, you'll have more choice about the jobs you take and the prices those clients are prepared to pay.

The rate at which quotations convert to paid work

Track not only requests to quote, but which ones convert to paid work. Traffic's great, but only if it ends up helping you to pay the bills!

The ratio of famine to feast

If you're an editor who's suffered periods of famine, keep an eye on any changes over time. Evaluate monthly, quarterly, annually – whichever suits. Once you find yourself in a position where you're having to turn more work down that you accept, you know your marketing's really working for you.

11. Does it work?

It's worked for me and everyone else I know who's committed to it. Commitment is the core of it. That doesn't mean you need to blog every day or every week. It *does* mean you need to build time into your business to create high-quality content on a regular basis. It is a lot of work, which is why I repurpose as much as I can, and recommend you do to.

I created a whopper of a post on how to punctuate dialogue in a novel. Here's how that's been repurposed in multiple ways so that I can squeeze every bit of business-worthy, client-attracting juice out of it:

- Turned the blog post into a PowerPoint slide deck, added a voiceover and created seven videos. Placed them on my YouTube channel.
- Created an ebooklet from the blog and placed that in my writing-resources library.
- Pulled the whole lot together and reframed it as a free mini course that I link to in my writing library and advertise on my training-courses page.
- Tweaked the blog post and used it as the foundation for a section in the chapter on dialogue in my book *Editing Fiction at Sentence Level* and in my guides *Making Sense of Punctuation* and *Making Sense of Dialogue*.
- Used it as the foundation of a small section in my multimedia self-study course Switching to Fiction.
- Linked to the blog in multiple editorial reports.

Blogging therefore works hard for us when we use the content in multiple ways, and keeps on working for us long after we've made the initial effort. And that's why I love it. Though it might appear to require a lot of work, in the end, it saves us time while it's making us visible.

I wish you every success with your own blogging journey, and look forward to seeing how you turn your words into other useful things that people will be grateful for, and might even pay for.

Tools and resources

- Bit.ly: URL shortener (useful analytics included): https://app.bitly.com
- Box Shot: Graphic-design tool (I find Box Shot 3D easier to use though it's now been retired and has no technical support. You'll need to enquire directly about the price): https://boxshot.com/
- Buffer: Social media scheduler: https://buffer.com
- BuzzSumo: Social media engagement and content analysis tool: https://app.buzzsumo.com
- Canva Copy Special: Free downloadable templates from Andrew and Pete: https://www.andrewandpete.com/how-to-create-social-media-graphics
- Canva: Graphic-design tool for non-designers: http://www.canva.com
- Click to Tweet: Promote, share and track your content on Twitter: https://clicktotweet.com
- Copyscape: Search for plagiarized website content and add banners to defend your site: http://copyscape.com
- CoSchedule Headline Analyzer: Tool for creating blog headlines: https://coschedule.com/headline-analyzer
- ConvertKit: Email marketing and blog-subscription management tool (not free): https://convertkit.com
- Emotional Marketing Value Headline Analyzer: Tool for creating blog headlines: http://aminstitute.com/headline
- Feedly: Content-curation tool: https://feedly.com
- Gifmaker.me: Gif-creation tool: http://gifmaker.me
- Giphy: Gif-creation tool: https://giphy.com
- Google Analytics: For some excellent guidance on getting the best from GA (and so much more), visit Andy Crestodina's excellent blog at Orbit Media Studios: https://www.orbitmedia.com/blog
- Google Slides: Slideshow tool that can be also used to create booklets: https://www.google.com/slides/about

- How to get the right visitors to your blog – the one with Amanda Webb: Atomic member-only content
- MailChimp: Mailing-list and blog-subscription management tool: https://mailchimp.com
- MoShow: Slideshow movie-maker app available from iTunes: https://moshowapp.com/. There's a great tutorial on how to use it via KPS Digital Marketing: 'How To Turn Photos Into Stunning Videos in Seconds': http://kpsdigitalmarketing.co.uk/2017/12/15/video-app-tutorial/
- Lumen5: Online video-creation tool that lets you repurpose blog posts: https://lumen5.com
- Ow.ly: URL shortener: http://ow.ly/url/shorten-url
- Raw Shorts: Drag-and-drop explainer video-animation tool (free and low-cost premium options): https://www.rawshorts.com
- Recurpost: Social media scheduler: https://recurpost.com
- Shareaholic: Social media sharing buttons: https://shareaholic.com
- StatCounter: Analytics tool: http://statcounter.com
- TinyPNG: Image compressor: https://tinypng.com
- Unsplash: Royalty-free images: https://unsplash.com
- Yellowpipe: Brand-colour converter (hex and RGB): http://www.yellowpipe.com/yis/tools/hex-to-rgb/color-converter.php
- Zoom: Slideshow recording and conferencing tool: https://zoom.us

Printed in Great Britain
by Amazon